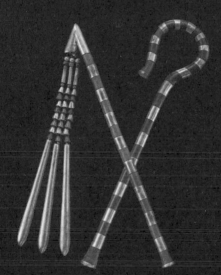

TUTANKHAMUN

THE MYSTERY OF THE BOY KING

by ZAHI HAWASS

Director of Excavations at the
Giza Pyramids and the
Valley of the Golden Mummies

NATIONAL GEOGRAPHIC
WASHINGTON, D.C.

Dedication To Dina

I have an eight-year-old Egyptian-American friend named Dina. Whenever she comes to Egypt, she also comes to visit me. We have had many adventures together now, and I think of her as a charm for good luck. I like to write about our adventures in my newspaper column, and she was part of my last children's book, *Curse of the Pharaohs*. Dina is becoming a symbol for American girls who want to become archaeologists. Kids her age write me letters all the time to say that archaeology is fun. Not long ago, I took Dina to a tomb at Saqqara (a place near Cairo where there are pyramids). This tomb was a shaft about thirty feet deep. We went down inside and watched as a coffin that had been sealed thousands of years ago was opened. Dina looked scared, and when it was opened, we found a mummy inside. Dina put her hands over her face and screamed, but little by little she took away her hands and began to smile.

∿∿∿∿∿∿∿∿∿∿∿∿∿∿∿∿∿∿∿∿∿∿∿∿∿∿∿∿∿∿

ACKNOWLEDGMENTS

I would like to thank many people who contributed to this book. First I would like to thank Dina and her class at the Warner School in Westwood, L.A. We had a wonderful discussion when I visited them recently, which gave me inspiration. Also, I would like to thank Nina Hoffman, head of the book division at the National Geographic, for encouraging me to write books for children. Thanks also to Kevin Mulroy for his support, and to Nancy Feresten for her hard work in editing this book. In addition, I would like to thank my assistant Mohamed Ismail, and Brook Myers, who is responsible for helping me answer all the letters that I receive from children. It always pleases me to see young people who want to become archaeologists. Last but not least, I would like to thank my colleague, Janice Kamrin, for editing and advising me on this book.

Library of Congress Cataloging-in-Publication Data

Hawass, Zahi A.
Tutankhamun : the mysteries of the boy king / Zahi Hawass.
p. cm.
Includes bibliographical references and index.
1. Tutankhamun, King of Egypt. 2. Egypt--History--Eighteenth dynasty, ca. 1570-1320 B.C. 3. Pharaohs--Biography. I. Title.
DT87.5.H39 2005
932'.014'092--dc22   2004015002

ISBN: 0-7922-8354-6 (trade hardcover edition)
ISBN: 0-7922-8355-4 (library edition)

Illustrations credits: Cover photograph by Kenneth Garrett. All inside photographs by Kenneth Garrett, except: p. 1, Antikenmuseum Basel/Andreas Voegelin; p. 6, © Corbis; p. 10, Photo by Kenneth Garrett, Art by Elisabeth Daynès; 12, Greg Reeder; 17, The Metropolitan Museum of Art; 18, © Stapleton Collection/Corbis; 23, Araldo de Luca/Archivo White Star; 28, © Roger Wood/Corbis; 30, © Reuters/ Corbis; 36, Erich Lessing/Art Resource, NY; 40-41, © Roger Wood/Corbis; 44, © Sandro Vannini/Corbis; 45, Victor R. Boswell, Jr.; 46, Art by Damnfx; 51, 52, CT Scanning Equipment provided by Siemens AG, data courtesy of Supreme Council of Antiquities, Arab Republic of Egypt, digital composite and coloration by NGM Art; 56, Art by Damnfx.

Text credit: p. 27. Translation from John L. Foster, Ancient Egyptian Literature. Austin: University of Texas Press, 2001, p. 2.

Captions:
FRONT COVER: The likeness of the boy king Tutankhamun shows on the face of a funerary statue, or shabti found in the pharaoh's tomb. Such statues were buried with important people to act as servants in the passage to the afterlife. PAGE 1, Pharaoh Tutankhamun's ceremonial crook (hega) and flail (nekhakha) are ancient Egyptian symbols of royal power. PAGE 2–3 The mask that covered the head and shoulders of the mummified King Tut.

HOWARD CARTER, KING TUT, AND ME

The discovery of the tomb of King Tutankhamun of Egypt was one of archaeology's greatest moments. I know how English archaeologist Howard Carter must have felt when he discovered the stairway leading to the tomb on a November morning in 1922. Of course, he must have been filled with excitement. At the same time, he must have been overcome by peace and silence. Imagine the moment, three weeks after the discovery, when he peered into the tomb itself for the first time and saw "everywhere the gleam of gold!" Perhaps he imagined that he could almost speak to the people who had buried the young king and surrounded him with precious gold more than 3,000 years earlier.

I can picture this scene so vividly because I, too, am an archaeologist. Like Carter, I have dedicated my life to the mysteries of ancient Egypt, and, like him, I have found tombs. I love exploring tunnels and dark shafts never knowing what I will find. Just before the lid of a new coffin is opened, I ask myself: "What is inside? Is it a mummy covered

Howard Carter (kneeling in front), his Egyptian overseer (in turban), and architect A.R. Callender, opening one of the gold-covered shrines that protected the sarcophagus of the King Tutankhamun.

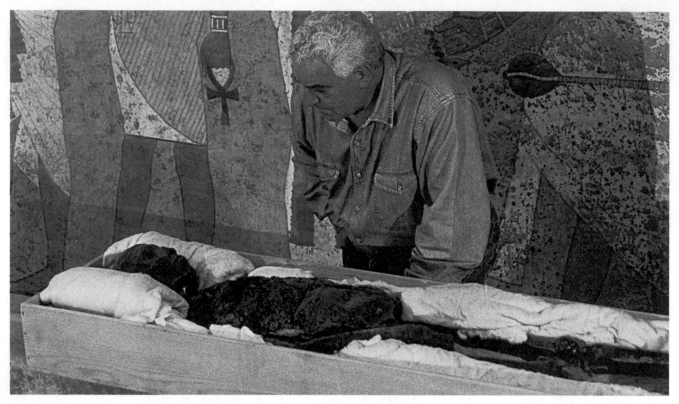

Here I am examining the mummy of Tutankhamun. The mummy rests where Howard Carter left him in 1926, in a wooden tray filled with sand inside the king's outermost coffin and his stone sarcophagus.

with precious amulets to protect the body with their magic, or is it empty, robbed long ago?" My heart beats faster and faster, until the lid is lifted and I see inside for the first time. When the mummy is there, I feel such excitement, and such happiness.

Those of us who study the ancient past like to think of ourselves as detectives, trying to solve mysteries that are thousands of years old. Like modern detectives, we search for clues. Many of these have disappeared over the course of time, but there are many still buried beneath the sand. The tomb of Tutankhamun was found almost intact, so we have more clues about him than about most other ancient Egyptian kings. But there are still many mysteries about his life and death that remain unsolved.

Howard Carter was a great archaeological detective. He was born in May 1874 in England. He first came to Egypt as an artist, to copy the scenes and hieroglyphics in some tombs. Afterwards, he went to work with Sir William Flinders Petrie, a famous English archaeologist. Petrie taught Carter how to excavate and introduced him to the scientific method. This meant that instead of just collecting things, he learned to keep a careful record of exactly where and how things were found. He also learned how to excavate without damaging what he found. This is the best way to both find and preserve as many clues as possible. Carter dedicated his life to archaeology. He made many important discoveries, but his greatest moment was when he discovered the tomb of King Tut.

In this book, I will tell you the story of Carter's great discovery, and then I

This map shows the places where King Tutankhamun lived and was buried, as well as some other famous sites in Egypt.

will tell you about the life and mysterious death of the Pharaoh Tutankhamun, the boy king who has captured the hearts of people around the globe. Come with me now as we journey to the past, first to November 1922 and then much farther, to the world of Egypt three thousand years ago.

CHAPTER ONE

THE GREAT
DISCOVERY

Before November 4, 1922, very little was known about King Tutankhamun. His name did not appear on any of the lists of kings left by the ancient Egyptians. But archaeologists did know that he existed because his name had been found on a number of objects. For example, a pit containing hundreds of statues was found in 1903 at Karnak, a huge complex of temples in what is now the modern city of Luxor. Some of these statues bore the name of Tutankhamun.

Luxor is the modern name for the ancient Egyptian city Waset. It is often called by its ancient Greek name, Thebes. It is located about 416 miles (670 kilometers) south of the modern city of Cairo and stretches across both banks of the Nile river.

During the first decade of the 20th century, archaeologists working for a rich American named Theodore Davis found some objects in the Valley of the Kings that

The face of Pharaoh Tutankhamun comes alive from the past with the help of modern technology. The lifelike recreation was sculpted based on images made by a machine called a CT scanner that allows researchers to see bones and tissue deep within the mummy.

belonged to King Tutankhamun. The Valley of the Kings is really two canyons (called *wadis* in Arabic) that cut through the cliffs on the west bank of the Nile River in what is now Luxor.

Kings in the Old and Middle Kingdom had been buried beneath huge pyramids, which made the tombs easy for thieves to find. So the pharaohs of the New Kingdom (from about 1550 to 1080 B.C.) hid their tombs in the cracks and crevices of the Valley of the Kings, hoping that tomb robbers would not be able to find them. By 1922, 61 tombs had been found in the Valley of the Kings, about 25 of which belonged to kings. (The other ones were either empty or belonged to other important people.) All of these tombs were found first by grave robbers, who stole most of their contents, and then by modern explorers and archaeologists. Egyptologists knew that Tutankhamun had lived during the New Kingdom, but they had not found his tomb.

The Valley of the Kings is a special place for me. I worked there in one of my first jobs as an archaeologist. An American team was excavating nearby, and it was my job to supervise them. During this time, I stayed at a hotel owned by a man named Sheikh Ali, four miles (six and a half kilometers) away from the Valley. Sheikh Ali was a member of the Abdou el-Rassoul family. This family has lived on the west bank of Thebes for many generations. Some think that they have lived there since the time of the pharaohs. Sheikh Ali was 70 when I met him in the 1970s, and he had known Howard Carter personally. He was present for the great discovery.

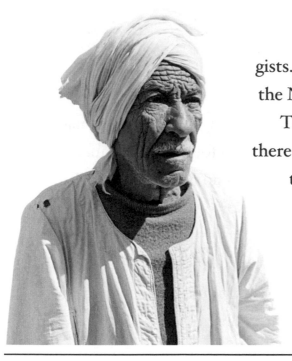

Sheikh Ali was a young man in 1922 and was there when Tutankhamun's tomb was discovered. He told me his stories personally when I was a young archaeologist working in Luxor.

A view of the famous Valley of the Kings from the air. The desolate valley was the resting place for most of the pharaohs of the New Kingdom, along with some especially favored members of their court. It is located on the west bank of the Nile across from the modern city of Luxor (ancient Thebes). The tombs are hidden in the valley floor, or high up in the cliffs.

I had just fallen in love with archaeology and wanted to be like Carter. To try to understand how he felt, I wanted to be alone in the Valley. During the day, thousands of tourists disturb it and change its silence. So one night, at midnight, I left the hotel. First I climbed up the cliff to see the spot where Sheikh Ali's family had discovered a group of royal mummies in the 1800s. Afterward, I continued over the cliffs to the Valley of the Kings, where

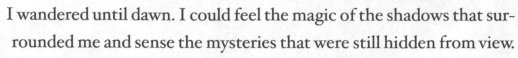

I wandered until dawn. I could feel the magic of the shadows that surrounded me and sense the mysteries that were still hidden from view. That night, I stood alone in front of the tomb of Ramses VI, who ruled Egypt 200 years after Tutankhamun. This tomb lies near the entrance to the Valley. The workmen who built this tomb lived at Deir el-Medina, on the other side of the cliffs. Each week they would come to stay in the Valley so that they could work hard on the king's tomb, and each weekend they would return home to their families.

The workmen didn't know it, but they had built their weekday huts above the spot where Tutankhamun was buried. No one (not even thieves) thought to look under the workers' huts for a tomb. This saved King Tut from robbers for more than 3,000 years, until Howard Carter came along.

A funerary statuette, or shabti, *crafted for Tutankhamun, along with 412 others of various sizes and shapes, made from many different materials. This figure once held a crook and a flail, symbols of royal power (see photo on page 1), but now has only his crook.*

Carter had been appointed the first chief inspector of antiquities for Upper Egypt in 1899. The area he was responsible for included the Valley of the Kings. Over the next five years, he got to know this area very well. In 1904, he was moved to the north of Egypt, to what was considered a more important job. But several months later, he had a fight with some very rude tourists. Carter was a stubborn man and refused to apologize to them. The director of the Antiquities Service had no choice but to fire him.

A few months later, Carter met Lord Carnarvon and agreed to work for him. Carnarvon was a wealthy Englishman who had come to Egypt for his health. He had been in a car accident as a young man (in one of the very first cars!) and had never completely recovered. At the time, Egypt was a British territory, and there were many English people living here. Carnarvon thought the sunny, dry climate of Egypt would do him good. His health improved, but he got bored. So, like many other rich foreigners of this era, he decided to take up excavating to keep himself occupied. He found that he was fascinated by Egypt's ancient past.

Many people had explored the Valley of the Kings. The tombs of almost all of the kings of the New Kingdom (the period when Tutankhamun lived) had been found. Many were missing their mummies, but amazingly many of the mummies of the kings had also been discovered.

During the period just after the end of the New Kingdom, several groups of priests, under orders from their rulers, opened every royal tomb they could find in the Valley of the Kings. They cleaned out most of what had not already been taken by tomb robbers and removed the royal mummies. Using an empty royal tomb as a workshop, they unwrapped each of the kings (and other royal family members buried with them) and took most of the amulets or precious objects that were still left. Then they wrapped the bodies up again and labeled them carefully. Scholars think that they did this partly because they needed valuable objects to pay for the burials of the new kings.

Statue of King Tut's ancestor Amenhotep II holding an offering table. Images of food such as meat and vegetables were carved onto the top of this table so that they would be magically available for eternity.

Most of the objects buried with the kings were taken away and melted down or reused by the new pharaohs. Under cover of night, the priests moved the royal mummies and some of the less valuable items, such as ancient scrolls called papyri and funerary statuettes called *shabtis,* to secret hiding places.

The first of these hiding places, or caches, was found sometime in the late 1800s by Sheikh Ali's family, who knew many of the secrets of the Valley. In a rock-cut tomb at Deir el-Bahri they found the bodies of ten kings and also some important queens. A second hiding place, the tomb of a king named Amenhotep II, was found in 1898 in the Valley of the Kings. There were 11 kings' mummies in this tomb. So between these two caches, the bodies of 20 of the 31 rulers of the New Kingdom had been found.

Thus, by 1914 almost all of the kings of the New Kingdom had been accounted for, either with a tomb, or a mummy, or both. But Tutankhamun remained an unsolved mystery. Archaeologists hadn't found his tomb, and, even stranger, they hadn't found his mummy. Carter thought that the tomb of Tutankhamun might still be hidden beneath the sands of the Valley of the Kings. He convinced Carnarvon that they should look for it.

Carter and Carnarvon began their excavations in the Valley of the Kings in 1917. After working for four seasons (each about three months long), they had found nothing of importance. Carnarvon called Carter to Highclere, his castle in England, and told him that he didn't want to spend any more money on a wild goose chase. Carter told him that there was one area of the Valley still unexplored. In the end, Carnarvon agreed to pay for one more season.

Carter arrived in Egypt in late October 1922. He knew that this was his last chance to discover the tomb. On November 1, he started work in the only place left to look, the area in front of the tomb of Ramses VI, where the workers' huts still stood. These structures were very important to archaeologists, so Carter had his men photograph, draw, and measure them and collect all the artifacts they could. Then he told them to clear the huts away. (This only took a few days. Modern archaeologists would take a lot longer because we are even more careful now.)

I asked Sheikh Ali, who had been an eyewitness, to tell me about the great discovery. He told me, "We sang all the time. My cousin was in charge of transporting the water jars to the site. The jars had pointed bottoms and had to be set into holes in the sand so they would stand up. On the morning of November 4, 1922, my cousin came with the water and began to dig a hole for the first jar. With his hand, he uncovered the top of a step cut into the rock. Without telling the Reis (the man in charge of the workmen), he ran back to the tent to tell Carter, so that he would get a reward.

"The workmen saw what was happening, and a hush fell over the Valley. My cousin came back with Carter and showed him the hole. Carter brushed away some more sand with his hand and said, 'This is

This photograph taken in the 1920s shows the large excavated entrance to the tomb of Ramses V and, in the bottom right-hand corner, the smaller entrance to the tomb of Tutankhamun.

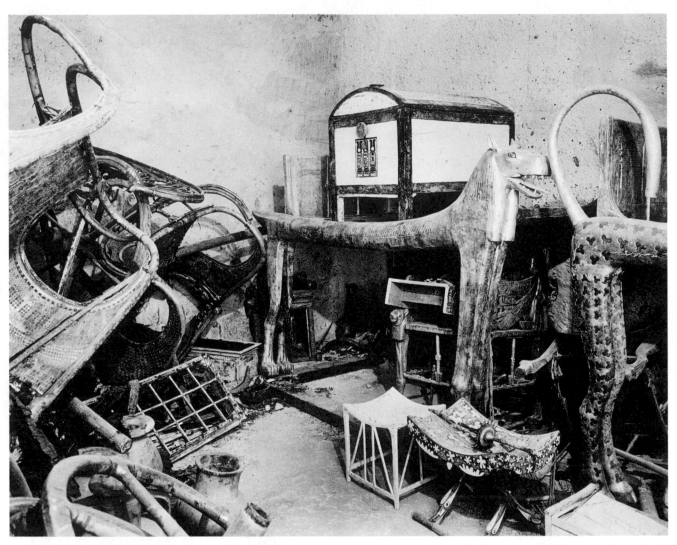

Carter already knew the tomb had been robbed before he entered this room because he could see evidence both on the blocking of the door and on the corridor leading down. The disorder of these treasures only confirmed what he had already figured out.

the tomb.' He had his workmen clear the stairway that led down below the bedrock. At the bottom was a blocked doorway. The plaster that covered the surface was stamped with the ancient seal of the necropolis (cemetery) guards: a jackal above nine captive enemies."

In great excitement, Carter set a guard to make sure that no one disturbed the area and ran back to his tent to send a telegram to Lord Carnarvon. It said: "At last have made wonderful discovery in Valley; a magnificent tomb with seals intact; re-covered same for your arrival; congratulations."

Lord Carnarvon and his daughter, Evelyn Herbert, arrived at the Valley on November 24, 1922. While they watched, Carter and his men finished clearing the doorway. They soon found the name of Tutankhamun, stamped onto the plaster.

The workers broke down the first door. Then they cleared the long rubble-filled passageway that lay behind it. At the end was another plastered doorway. Carter knew that the tomb lay just beyond.

Late in the afternoon of November 26, Carter made a small hole in the doorway. He lit a candle, and put it inside to test the air. Then he made the hole bigger so he could look inside. Carnarvon, who was standing beside him and asked anxiously, "What do you see?"

Carter, his eyes shining in the candlelight, answered, "Wonderful things!"

There were four chambers in the tomb. Each of these was crammed full of fabulous objects—of gold, wood, precious stone, and pottery. More than 5,000 artifacts were there, tangled together in jumbled heaps. The mummy of Tutankhamun was in the burial chamber, inside a nest of coffins and shrines.

Carter and a team of experts wrote down, drew, and photographed exactly where and how each object was found and moved each one very carefully so that nothing would be damaged. Recording and moving all of the objects took them ten years.

Archaeologists are still studying the objects that Howard Carter found, along with other monuments and artifacts from other places in Egypt that date from the same period. Using all of these clues, scholars are trying to piece together the story of the boy king. Let us now continue our journey back to ancient Egypt, to the world of Tutankhamun.

CHAPTER TWO

EGYPT BEFORE TUTANKHAMUN

Tutankhamun was born during the Golden Age of Egypt, another name for the New Kingdom. This was a time when Egypt was very rich and powerful and controlled a large empire. Most scholars believe that Tutankhamun was the grandson of Amenhotep III, the ninth king of the New Kingdom.

Amenhotep III was a powerful king. He ruled over an Egypt whose empire stretched far to the north and south. In his time, the land was at peace. A queen named Tiye was Amenhotep III's main wife. She was a very powerful woman, and I believe that the king loved her very much. I think this because he mentions her often in inscriptions, and she is sometimes shown the same size as her husband in statues. Amenhotep III and Tiye had at least two sons: Tuthmosis, who died young, and Amenhotep.

A colossal (bigger than life-size) statue of Amenhotep IV, thought to be Tutankhamun's father. This king chose the sun disk, called the Aten, as his most important god, and changed his name, which meant "Amun is Satisfied," to Akhenaten, "Blessed Spirit of the Aten," to honor his god. He and his wife Nefertiti built a city for their god at a site now called Amarna.

For thousands of years, the ancient Egyptians had worshiped many gods, including Thoth, god of wisdom, Hathor, goddess of love and beauty, and Osiris, god of the dead. The king of the gods was Re, the sun god. Ancient Egyptians showed their gods as humans, as animals, or as humans with animal heads. The Egyptians did not really think their gods were animals. They worshiped characteristics of certain animals—for example their intelligence or their strength—that they associated with the gods.

During the New Kingdom, the most important god was Amun, which can also be written Amen or Amon. This god was from Thebes, the ancestral home of the royal family. When this royal family took over Egypt, Amun became their official god, and many of them (like Amenhotep), included him in their names.

A great temple to this god, who was often combined with the sun god to become Amun-Re, was built on the east bank of the Nile in Thebes. This temple was called Karnak. A smaller temple to Amun, now known as Luxor Temple, was built several miles to the south, still in Thebes. Amenhotep III did a great deal of building in both of these temples and at many other temples all over Egypt. He was very religious and built monuments dedicated to many different gods.

Ancient Egyptian kings were thought of as somewhere between human and divine. They were responsible for taking care of the gods and for talking to them. Most kings do not seem to have been thought of as gods themselves until after they died.

Statue of the falcon-headed god Horus. Horus was a god of the sky and the sun. He was also the son of the king of the dead, Osiris. He was the patron of the living pharaoh and protected him from harm.

Every king who ruled at least 30 years celebrated something called a Sed festival, which was supposed to show everyone that he was still young enough and strong enough to be in charge. After his first Sed festival, a king could have others as often as he wanted. At his first Sed festival (he had three all together), Amenhotep III declared himself a god. After this, he had his artists show him as many different Egyptian gods.

Some scholars think that the younger Amenhotep started ruling beside his father before his father died, but others think that he didn't become king until Amenhotep III's death. Either way, when he began his reign, he was called Amenhotep IV.

When he first became king, Amenhotep IV would have had a palace at Memphis, in the north of Egypt, and another at Thebes. He built temples to his favorite god, the Aten, near the temple of Amun at Karnak.

The Aten was the sun disk, and the name Aten simply means "sun disk." Instead of being represented as a human or an animal, the Aten was shown as a circle, as the globe of the sun itself. This god was also very important to Amenhotep III, who called himself "the dazzling Aten." Some people think that Amenhotep IV worshiped his own father as the Aten.

From the beginning of his reign, Amenhotep IV had himself portrayed with a very long narrow face, a big chin, slanted eyes, and thick lips. He is shown with a long torso and very wide hips, a sagging belly, breasts, and long, skinny legs.

The jackal head of Anubis watched over the tomb of Tutankhamun. Anubis, one of the gods of the dead, was in charge of mummification. He helped people who had died to complete their dangerous journeys from death to eternal life.

A bove: Akhenaten worships the sun disk, the Aten, with Queen Nefertiti. During the reign of this king, the Aten was shown as the globe of the sun, its streaming rays ending in hands that hold out the symbol of life (the ankh) to the royal family. Background: Sun sets over the Nile River near the Valley of the Kings.

Some people think that he didn't really look like this but had himself shown this way for religious reasons. One theory suggests that he wanted to be seen as a fertility god. These sorts of gods are usually shown with sagging bellies, breasts, and wide hips. He also might have wanted to be seen as both male and female. This could have been a way of showing that he was like a god who had aspects of many different gods within his own body. Other people think he really did look this way and might have been born with a disease called Marfan syndrome. People with this disease look similar in many ways to pictures and statues of Amenhotep IV. They tend to be tall, with long arms and legs and faces. They are also usually near-sighted, and some people have suggested that Amenhotep IV loved the sun so much because it helped him see.

In the fifth year of his reign, Amenhotep IV changed his name to Akhenaten, "Blessed Spirit of the Aten," to honor his favorite god. At about the same time, he decided to leave Thebes for a new city that he had been building. This city was in the middle of Egypt, built mostly in the desert but close to the river Nile.

He called his new city Akhetaten, "the Horizon of the Aten." Scholars usually call it Amarna, which is its modern name. Akhenaten chose this place for many reasons. One of these was that no other gods had been worshiped there, so it was spiritually pure. Some scholars now think that the Black

A statue of Akhenaten holding an offering table. This statue was found in the house of one of the king's subjects. Since only the royal family could worship the Aten directly, statues of the king or queen were set up in shrines in people's houses so they could communicate with the god.

Plague had come to Egypt and that Akhenaten wanted to get his family and courtiers away from the disease.

Akhenaten believed that he and his family were the only ones who had direct communication with the Aten. All others had to worship the Aten through him, his wife Nefertiti, and their daughters. He had his artists show the Aten with rays streaming from it. At the ends of the rays were human hands that stretched out the ankh sign, the hieroglyph for life, to the king and his family.

At some point in his reign, Akhenaten stopped worshipping Amun and many other gods. He is said to have closed the temples of Amun, and we know that he had the name of this god hacked out wherever his workmen could find it. Even though he was the king, this was a very brave thing to do since the priests of Amun were very powerful and very rich. Can you imagine how upset those priests must have been?

Some people still worshiped other gods, but the Aten was by far the most important. Akhenaten himself thought that all other gods were just aspects of the Aten. Many people think that Akhenaten was the first monotheist (which means that he worshiped only one god), in history. His new religion was a very big change, and it probably made many people very unhappy. But both the king and his family loved the Aten. Akhenaten even wrote a beautiful poem to the Aten. Here is the beginning:

> Let your holy Light shine from the height of heaven,
> O living Aten, source of all life!
> From eastern horizon risen and streaming,
> You have flooded the world with your beauty...
> Though you are far, your light is wide upon earth;
> and you shine in the faces of all
> who turn to follow your journeying.

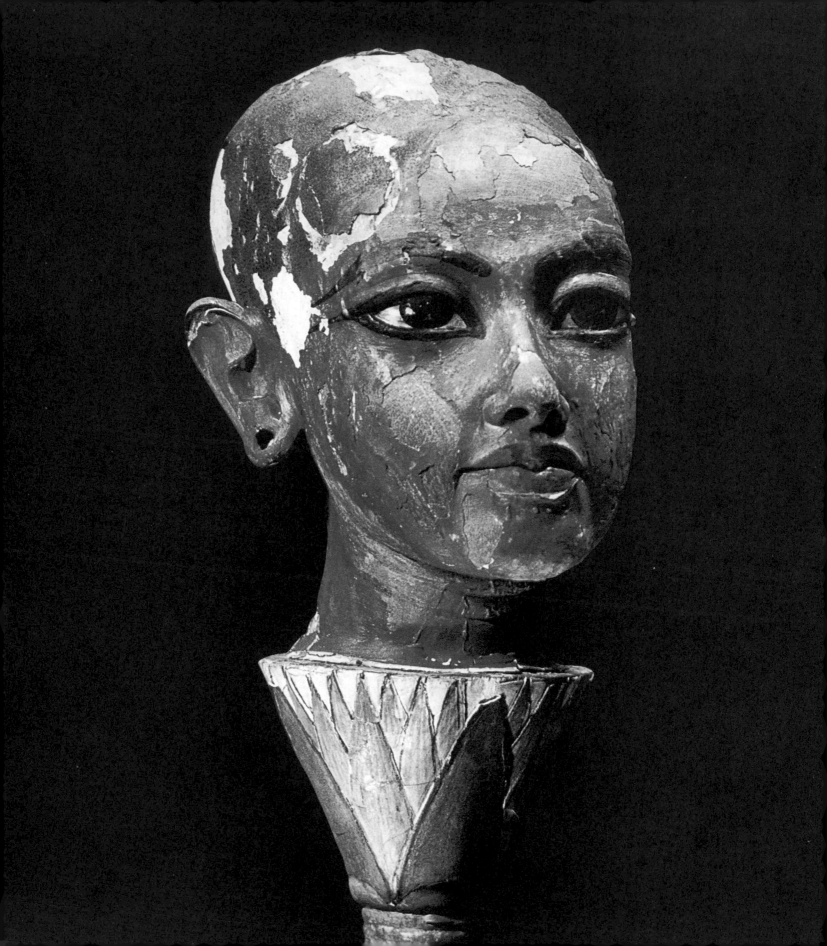

CHAPTER THREE

TUTANKHAMUN
KING OF EGYPT

Kings of Egypt could have more than one wife, and Akhenaten was no exception. His most important queen was Nefertiti. We know from some of her portraits that she was a very beautiful woman, and many scholars think that she ruled beside her husband. Akhenaten and Nefertiti had six daughters, who are shown with them in many ancient pictures. Akhenaten had another important wife named Kiya.

We believe that Tutankhamun was born in the 11th or 12th year of Akhenaten's reign. We know that he was the son of a king, but we do not know for sure who his parents were. I believe that he was the son of Akhenaten and Kiya. Queen Kiya disappeared at about the time of his birth, so if she was his mother, she may have died in childbirth.

Tutankhamun was probably born at Amarna. He was originally named Tutankhaten (which means "living image of the Aten") and probably lived in a royal palace north of the

Tutankhamun, shown as a young child emerging from a lotus blossom. Lotuses close at night and open at dawn, so the Egyptians linked them with the rising sun. One name for the sun god at dawn was Nefertem, so this statue shows Tutankhamun as Nefertem.

center of the city. He was cared for by a woman named Maya. We know about Maya because her tomb was found by a French archaeologist named Alain Zivie. A beautiful scene in her tomb shows the king sitting on her lap.

When Tutankhaten was about five, Akhenaten died. We do not know how he died. If he did have Marfan Syndrome, he might have died young because of his disease. Some people believe that he was killed by the priests of Amun, but there aren't any clues to tell us that. Either a king named Smenkhkare or Nefertiti became the ruler for a few years, and then he or she died too.

The end of Akhenaten's reign and the few years after his death are still shrouded in a great deal of mystery, and no one is quite sure what happened. For example, we don't really have any idea who Smenkhkare was. Since he was a king, we assume he was a male member of the royal family and was probably Akhenaten's brother or son, but we don't really know that for sure.

The one thing we are certain about is that Tutankhaten became king a few years after Akhenaten's death. We think that he was only about eight or nine years old at the time. Since the new king was so young, the commander of the army, Horemheb, became his regent, the person who ruled for him while he was growing up. Another very important official who helped him a

A limestone statue of a woman holding a child. She is probably the child's nurse. This statue has no names written on it, so we don't know who the people are. However, it shows the sort of relationship that Tutankhamun would have had with Maya.

lot was a man named Ay. Some people think that Ay was the brother of Queen Tiye, Akhenaten's mother.

When Tut became king, he may already have been married to his queen, Ankhsenpaaten, the third oldest daughter of Akhenaten and Nefertiti. She would probably have been his half sister.

In ancient Egypt, it was normal for a king to marry his sister or half sister, even though regular people never did so. Some kings even married their daughters. There were practical reasons for keeping marriages in the family—by marrying each other, the royal family could keep power and wealth to themselves. But it was also because kings and queens were thought to be like gods and goddesses, who often married their brothers and sisters. For example, in Egyptian mythology, Nut, the goddess of the sky, married her brother Geb, the god of the earth. They had four children: Isis, Nephthys, Osiris, and Seth. Isis married Osiris, and Nephthys married Seth.

When Tutankhaten became king, there was a huge celebration called a coronation where he would have been presented with many crowns. The most important were the red crown, the white crown, the double crown, the blue crown, and the nemes headdress.

I can imagine the coronation, the ceremony at which Tutankhaten would have worn his crowns for the first time. Each of the crowns he wore had a special meaning. Egypt was divided into two parts: the north, or Lower Egypt, and the south, or Upper Egypt. When he wore the red crown, he was king of Lower Egypt. When he wore the white crown, he was king of Upper Egypt. When he wore the double crown, which was the white crown and the red crown together, it meant that he was king of a united land, in which Upper and Lower Egypt were one. Even though he was a child, he could wear the blue crown, also sometimes called the war helmet, which maybe meant that he was the leader of the army. Most of the time, Tutankhaten probably wore the nemes headdress, a striped cloth that fell over his shoulders.

All of his crowns would have had a cobra on the front. The cobra represents the goddess Wadjet. She was the goddess of Lower Egypt, and her job was to protect the king. Some crowns also had a vulture. This was Nekhbet, the goddess of Upper Egypt. In his hands, the king would have carried the crook and the flail. The crook showed that he was a shepherd to his people, and the flail meant that he was strong. The small crook and flail that the child Tutankhaten probably carried at his coronation were found in his tomb.

Each Egyptian king had five names. One he was given at birth, and the rest were given to him when he came to the throne. Tutankhamun's birth name was Tutankhaten. His throne name was Nebkheperure. When these names were carved onto walls or drawn onto furniture or other objects, they were written inside oval rings called cartouches, which symbolized the path of the sun through the sky. His other names were very long and were not used very often.

About two years after he became king, Tutankhaten changed his birth name to Tutankhamun. Ankhsenpaaten changed her name to Ankhsenamun. Before, the names of the king and queen had honored the Aten. Now they honored Amun. We don't know whether the boy king wanted to go back to the old religion or whether someone else—maybe Horemheb or Ay—forced him to do it. Even though Tutankhamun restored the old gods, he continued to worship the Aten as one among many.

This large box is decorated with the name of the king: Tutankhamun, ruler of Upper Egyptian Heliopolis (another name for Thebes). Inside were several crooks and flails and some jewelry, along with many other things.

The priesthood of Amun became powerful again. The temples to Amun in Thebes were reopened, and Tutankhamun built new monuments in them. After a few years, the city of Amarna was left behind. The king lived mostly at Memphis, and the court traveled to Thebes for religious festivals.

The main job of the young king was to keep the country stable and make sure everyone was safe by keeping his army ready to defend the country. He was also responsible for maintaining the temples and keeping the gods happy. This was a big job for a child, so he was helped by Horemheb and Ay. He also had two viziers, the highest officials in the government, who were in charge of Upper and Lower Egypt, and other important officials to serve him.

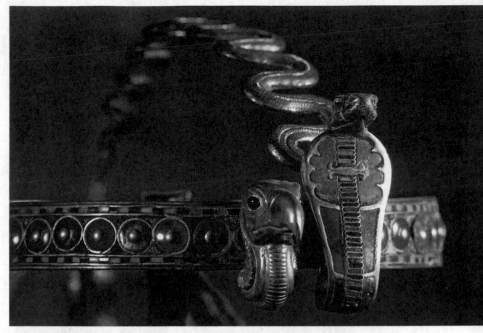

This crown was found on the head of King Tut's mummified body. On the front is the royal insignia, a vulture and a serpent, emblems of the two kingdoms over which Tut reigned.

Since Egypt was so rich, it was important to have people in charge of the treasuries where the wealth of the country was stored. One of Tutankhamun's treasurers was named Maya. He was also an overseer of construction, which meant he was in charge of building structures such as temples. He would mostly have made sure that everyone else was doing their job. Like the Maya who took care of Tut, Maya the treasurer, along with Horemheb and some of Tutankhamun's other important officials, built beautiful tombs for themselves at Saqqara, near Memphis.

Tutankhamun and Ankhsenamun would have lived a life of luxury, and I believe that they loved each other very much. Archaeologists have found clues in several places: at Memphis, at Thebes, at other sites, and especially in Tutankhamun's tomb. These clues tell us many things about the lives of the young couple.

CHAPTER FOUR

THE LIFE OF THE
BOY KING

The palaces where the young king and queen were raised would have been built of mud brick with beautifully painted walls and floors. Some pieces of walls and floors from the palaces at Amarna have been found by archaeologists. One floor is decorated with a garden scene. There is a rectangular pool alive with fish and surrounded by water plants. Calves play and ducks fly out of clumps of vegetation.

I like to imagine the young couple enjoying their lives together at Amarna or at the palace of Malqata, which was built by Amenhotep III on the west bank of Thebes, near the Valley of the Kings. Tutankhamun and Ankhsenamun would have stayed there when they went to Thebes for religious festivals. There was a huge lake in front of this palace, and Tutankhamun and Ankhsenamun might have gone boating there, perhaps taking a picnic with them to enjoy as they relaxed on the water. No palace from this era has been

A gilded throne inlaid with semiprecious stones from Tutankhamun's tomb. The young king sits on a throne under the rays of the Aten. Queen Ankhsenamun, wearing a fine linen dress and an elaborate crown, anoints her husband with perfume.

found at Memphis, but there must have been one, and it was probably very similar to the palace at Thebes.

Many baskets and boxes of food were found in Tutankhamun's tomb, so we have an idea of what he liked to eat. There were many different kinds of bread and cakes, and even wheat and barley to make more. Some of this grain might have been used to make beer, which Egyptians drank every day. However, there was no actual beer in the tomb. There was fruit juice and wine, so maybe Tutankhamun liked fruit juice and wine better than beer.

Many pieces of painted walls were found at Amarna, in the palaces that belonged to the royal family. They are covered with scenes showing the beauty of the natural world. Here are ducks flying out of clumps of marsh plants.

There was a lot of meat stored in egg-shaped wooden boxes—beef, part of a sheep or goat, and a lot of duck and goose meat. The king liked vegetables, too: there were chickpeas, lentils, and peas. To spice the royal food, the chefs used juniper berries, coriander, fenugreek, sesame, and black cumin, all of which were found in the tomb. For dessert, Tutankhamun brought along honey and dates, raisins, figs, jujubes, and various other fruits. There were also almonds and seeds.

There was a great deal of linen clothing in the tomb, some of it plain and some of it beautifully decorated with beads, embroidery, and even sequins. There were shirts and longer tunics, kilts, sashes, and even underwear. There were many pairs of sandals, some from when King Tut was a child and some from when he was older. The soles of some of the sandals were decorated with captives so that every time the king took a step, he could walk on the enemies of Egypt. There were also several pairs of gloves, as well as caps and headdresses.

Sunrise over the ancient ruins of the city of Amarna, capital city of Akhenaten. This is one of the temples to the Aten. In the distance is a model of the kind of column that would have filled this temple. It was set up by Barry Kemp, a British archaeologist who works at the site.

Painted ivory board game known as "20 squares," found in Tutankhamun's tomb.

Pictures of the king show him with wide hips and a bit of a belly, and he is often shown slouching. However, many people from the Amarna and post-Amarna periods (the time from the reign of Akhenaten through Tutankhamun and his successors) are shown in a similar way, so we cannot assume that he was shaped this way just from the pictures. On the other hand, scholars have studied his skeleton and his clothing and have determined that he was about 5 and a half feet (1.6 meters) tall and was pear-shaped, with a narrow waist and wide hips.

Some of Tutankhamun's writing equipment was found in his tomb. This included several palettes where he stored his reed pens and his black and red inks, a fancy case for more pens, a burnisher for polishing papyrus, and a water dish.

Some of the objects in Tutankhamun's tomb tell us about the love between the king and his queen. Perhaps the most famous is the Golden Throne. On the throne's back, inlaid in semiprecious stones and glass, is a picture. On one side, Tutankhamun sits on a throne, an elaborate (and very heavy) crown on his head. Ankhsenamun stands before him, a cup filled with scented oil in her hand. With one hand, she reaches out to anoint her husband.

Another important object from the tomb is a small golden shrine that might once have held a statue. Only the tiny footprints of this statue were inside the shrine when Carter found it, engraved onto a small base. The outside of the shrine is decorated with scenes that show Tutankhamun and Ankhsenamun together in the papyrus marshes. In one scene, the king pours liquid into his queen's hand while she sits at his feet; in another, she hands him arrows while he sits in a chair and shoots at some ducks; and in another, she fastens a collar around his neck. I think the king and queen must have loved to spend time together outdoors, enjoying the beautiful weather of Egypt.

Several board games were found in the king's tomb, so we think that the royal couple liked to play them. There was a Senet board, which has 30 squares. Each player had seven pieces, which he or she tried to get off the board first. Another game was called Twenty Squares (even though it really has 24 squares). For this game, which might have been a little bit like modern Parcheesi, each player had five pieces. Instead of dice, the royal couple and their friends would have used flat sticks. The player would spin or throw these and move according to the side on which they landed.

All of the instruments found in the tomb had important religious or official purposes although Tutankhamun and Ankhsenamun may have enjoyed music as well. Two trumpets might have been used on military occasions. Ivory clappers and sistra (a sistrum is a kind of musical rattle) were used in religious ceremonies.

Two tiny babies were found buried with Tutankhamun, each in its own miniature coffin. The first baby had died after five months inside her mother, four months before she should have been born. The other seems to have had a number of things wrong with her and died at birth. Most scholars believe that these are the children of Tutankhamun and Ankhsenamun. If there was a gene for Marfan syndrome in the family, it may have had something to do with why the babies died. I think that the king and queen must have been very sad when they lost their babies.

Many of the objects in the tomb of Tutankhamun tell us that the young king was interested in sports. There are bows and arrows in all sizes, shields, chariots, throwsticks (used for hunting birds), and even slingshots. All princes and kings were trained in war-related sports because if there was a war, they would have had to lead their troops into battle.

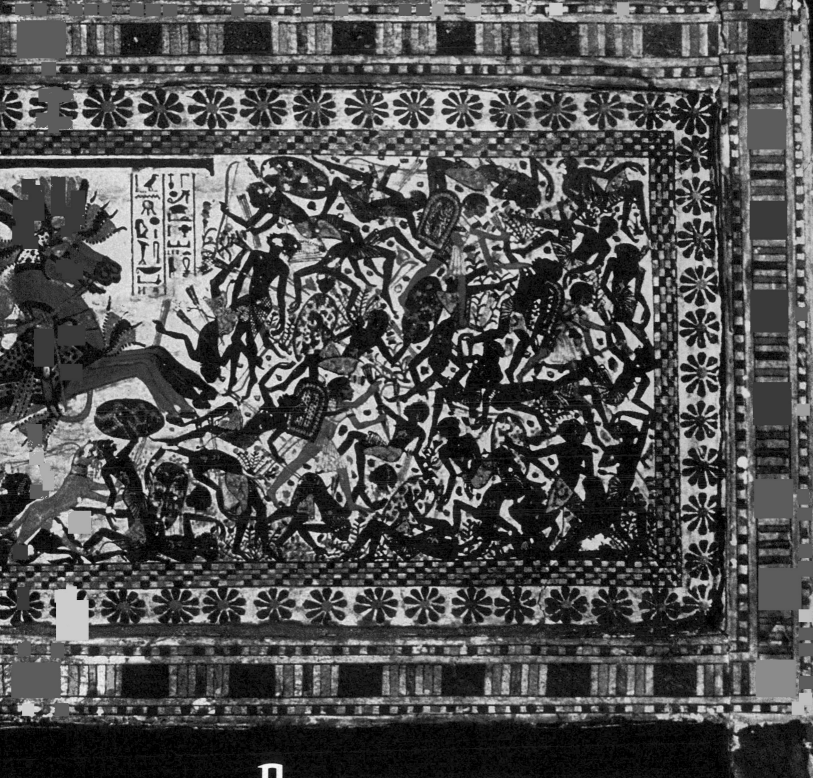

P ainted chest found in Tutankhamun's tomb. This side shows
Tutankhamun trampling Nubians under the wheels of his chariot.

The pyramids at Giza, in the desert near the ancient capital city of Memphis. A rest house belonging to Tutankhamun was found near one of the temples here. The king would have come to the area for hunting and military training.

Royal training took place near the ancient city of Memphis, in the north of Egypt. The training ground was in the desert near the pyramids of Giza and Saqqara. (The pyramids were already a thousand years old in the time of King Tut.) In ancient times, the desert was full of wild animals, including bulls, antelope, gazelles, and even lions. The area was called the Valley of the Gazelles.

Tutankhamun had a villa at Giza, where he could stay when he was training in the desert. My team recently found some very interesting evidence of the sorts of things

Tutankhamun and the other kings used to do, carved on some ancient blocks from the area where Tutankhamun had his training. One scene shows a trainer standing beside a prince. The prince holds a bow, and the trainer says, "Shoot at the target! Do not miss." Other scenes show people wrestling and fighting with sticks, activities that were also part of military training.

The many bows found in Tutankhamun's tomb are of various sizes, from child-size to bigger than Tut himself. There are different kinds also—straight bows from a single piece of wood and composite bows made of layers of different kinds of wood. Composite bows are more powerful than straight bows.

The young king would have practiced shooting with his bows and would have taken his horse and chariot into the desert to chase wild game. A golden fan from his tomb shows Tutankhamun hunting ostriches. On one side, he is shooting at them from his chariot. On the other side, he is coming home with the ostriches he has killed. The feathers from these ostriches would have been used for fans.

Hunting was practice for war. The Egyptian king was supposed to lead his army himself, from his chariot, so he had to be very good at riding in a chariot and shooting arrows at the same time. It is very hard to shoot straight when both you and your target are moving, so he needed a lot of practice.

This ceremonial shield shows Tutankhamun using a special curved sword called a scimitar to kill lions.

There is a story about Tutankhamun's ancestor, King Amenhotep II. When Amenhotep II was a child, he too used to train in the desert near Giza. He loved to ride horses and jump them over obstacles. The people in the court were scared that he would hurt himself, so they told his father, King Tuthmosis III. But Tuthmosis III, who was a great warrior king, just laughed and said he was glad his son was so brave. Maybe Tutankhamun had so much sports and battle equipment in his tomb because he was, or at least wanted to be, like his brave ancestor.

There are many objects from the tomb of Tutankhamun that show the king hunting wild animals or defeating enemies. For example, a beautiful painted box shows the king in his chariot. On top he is hunting animals, and on the sides he is fighting against Nubians (from the south) and Asiatics (from the northeast). Even though we think that Tutankhamun actually went hunting and maybe even went to war, the pictures alone cannot tell us for certain. This is because the pictures are not necessarily images of reality but have an important symbolic meaning.

In Egyptian mythology, the world was created from endless darkness and water. This was chaos, and even after the world was created, chaos was always there, surrounding and threatening the world. One of the king's jobs was to keep the world safe from chaos. Wild animals and enemies represented the forces of chaos. So when the king was shown hunting animals and fighting enemies, it meant he was fighting chaos and protecting the world.

While Amenhotep III and Akhenaten were alive, the great Egyptian empire had been mostly at peace with its neighbors. Its principal allies had been the Mitanni, who, like the Egyptians, had built an empire. Their heartland, called Naharin, lay to the north of the Euphrates River in what is now Syria. In the early New Kingdom, the Egyptians and the Mitanni had fought one another because both wanted to control the lands that lay between them. Amenhotep III's father, Tuthmosis IV, had made peace with the Mitanni. Both he and Amenhotep III had Mitanni princesses as wives.

During King Tutankhamun's lifetime, the world began changing very quickly. Sometime either during his reign or just before, people called the Hittites, who lived in what is now Turkey, attacked the Mitanni and took over their empire. Then the Hittites attacked the Egyptian empire. Egypt was involved in a serious war for the first time in almost 50 years, and its king was still less than 18 years old.

The inner soles of these sandals, found in Tutankhamun's tomb, picture Egypt's enemies. The king symbolically crushed them each time he took a step.

CHAPTER FIVE

DEATH AND
BURIAL

When the Hittites attacked the Egyptian empire, we think that Horemheb, as commander in chief of the army, had to go north to try and stop them. It was probably while he was gone that Tutankhamun died. We do not know what killed him.

We can sometimes tell how an ancient Egyptian died by studying his or her mummy. For example, we know that one king that ruled just before the beginning of the New Kingdom died in battle against enemies from the northeast. The marks of their battle axes can be seen on his skull. Now, we can use modern methods such as X rays and CT scans, which let us see inside mummies without damaging them. Sometimes we can see the effects of diseases, and even the organisms that caused them, inside mummies.

Tutankhamun's body has not been able to tell us very much about how he died. It is possible that he died of a disease, but we have no evidence for this. Some people think

This illustration reveals paintings with magical powers that adorn the walls of Tut's burial chamber. Most of the pictures show stages of Tut's dangerous trip to the afterworld. Baboons on the far wall represent the start of his passage through the 12 hours of the night, a journey symbolized by a boat bearing a scarab, emblem of the sun god.

that he was murdered, because some old X rays seem to show a place on the back of his skull that might be damage from a blow. According to one Egyptologist, named Bob Brier, someone might have snuck up on Tutankhamun, maybe in the middle of the night, and hit him on the head. He doesn't think that the king died right away and believes that he might even have gotten better for a while. But he thinks that maybe the doctors were afraid to treat him, because if they failed, they might be blamed for the king's death. So Tutankhamun was left to die. Brier also thinks that the person responsible was Ay, since he was the next king.

Many people disagree with this theory and think that the king died of natural causes. Even if the X ray and the reading of it were right, the king could have hurt his head in an accident. Fortunately, we have now done a new study of the mummy of Tutankhamun, so we know whether this theory is right or not.

On January 5, 2005, I traveled to Luxor to visit King Tutankhamun. Several days before, a big trailer had driven from Cairo to Luxor with a very special machine inside. This machine is called a CT scanner, or CAT scanner. An X-ray machine can only take one picture at a time, and we have to move the body every time we want to take a new one. With a CT scanner, we can take many photos at a time and then put them together in a computer to make a three-dimensional image of the body. With the CT scanner, we can see inside the mummy and look at details about things like bones and soft tissues. We can even find out a lot about what he might have looked like.

The afternoon when I went to the Valley of the Kings was gray and cloudy. It was about 4:30, and the tourists were all leaving for the day. A little while after we arrived, there was a huge rainstorm, and people began to worry about how we would get the king safely from his tomb to the machine. I went into Tut's tomb and opened the lid of his sarcophagus and coffin. The moment when I gazed on the face of the boy king is one I will never forget. I knew I was looking into the face of history.

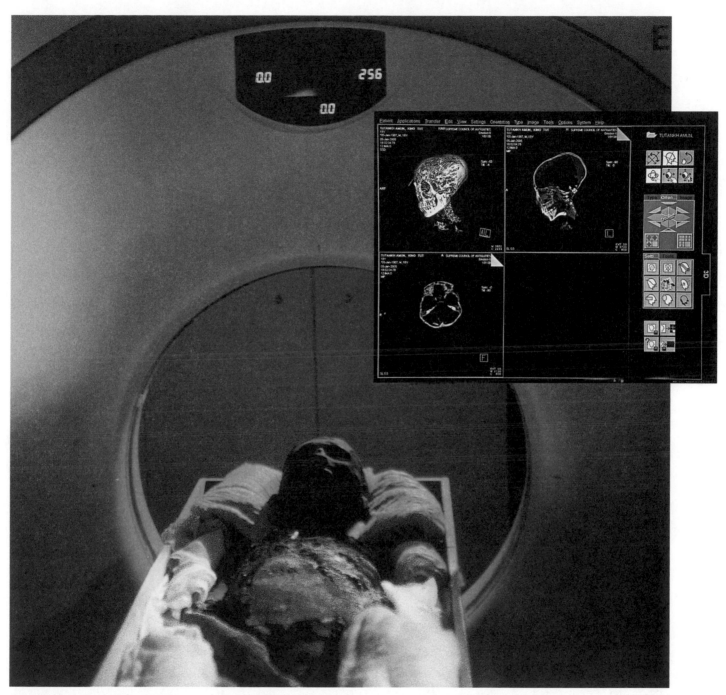

The mummy of Tutankhamun is introduced into a CT scanner for imaging. The inset photo shows views of Tut's head produced by the scanner.

We carefully took the mummy out of its coffin, where Carter had left it long ago. Fortunately, the rain stopped, so we took the body to the machine and laid it inside. We were all very excited, hoping we would learn something new. But then the machine wouldn't work! The fan that cooled it had stopped. Some people brought plastic fans from the town nearby, and we let them blow on the machine until it started to work again. In less than an hour, there were over 1,700 images stored inside the computer, to be studied later by experts. We put Tutankhamun back into his tomb, and then I returned to Cairo.

For the next two months, a team of Egyptian scientists and doctors studied the images. At the very end, another team of three scientists came from Italy and Switzerland. On March 4th and 5th, all of the scientists got together to talk about their finds.

Tutankhamun was not murdered by a blow to the head. There is no evidence anywhere on his mummy of foul play. This does not mean for sure that he was not murdered, but if he was, his mummy cannot tell us. Maybe we can find out more from his stomach and intestines, or lungs and liver. These were taken out of his body when he was made into a mummy and stored separately. But no one hit him on the back of the head.

The scientists who worked with Carter thought that Tutankhamun was between 18 and 22 when he died. The new team agrees; they think he was about 19. They know this from looking carefully at his bones and teeth. Tutankhamun was generally very healthy. He had always eaten well and hadn't had any terrible diseases. His teeth were in excellent shape, too. The scientists were surprised to find that he had a small cleft in his palette, which means that the roof of his mouth hadn't grown together quite right. They also found that he had one wisdom tooth that was impacted, meaning that it was stuck and couldn't come out. This might have been painful, but it would not have killed him.

The CT scan did show that something very bad might have happened to Tutankhamun right before he died. His left leg, just above the knee, was broken, and his left kneecap was detached. The scientists think this probably happened before he died, but it's possible that the embalmers (who made him into a mummy) or Carter's team, which handled the body very roughly, broke the leg. If it did happen before he died, it was a few days at the most, because it didn't have time to start healing.

Tutankhamun wouldn't have died just from a broken leg. But a wound over the break might have gotten infected, and infections can kill. He might also have had other injuries that can't be seen in bones.

The CT scan solved some important mysteries for us and also gave us new information to work with. For now, I think that Tutankhamun had an accident, but maybe we will find out something new in the future.

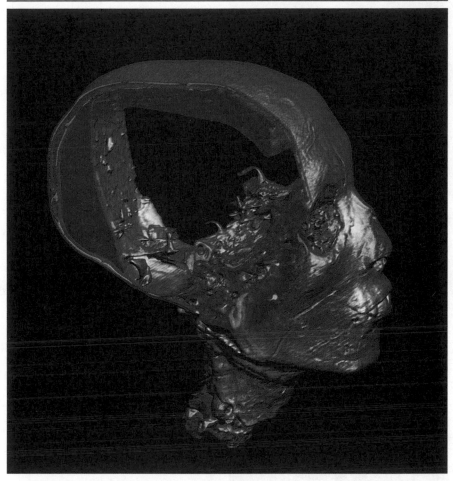

A three-dimensional image, made from the CT scan, which shows a slice of Tutankhamun's skull. The embalmers removed his brain and poured in embalming material. This material is now stuck to the top and back of the inside of his skull.

Tutankhamun had no sons, so many people think that Horemheb should have become the next king. But we know that the next king was Ay. It is possible that Ay took over because Horemheb was away fighting the Hittites. It is also possible that Ay was

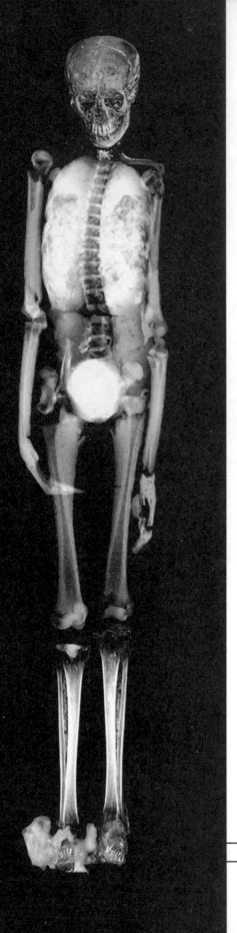

supposed to be the next king because he was Tutankhamun's closest living male relative.

Tutankhamun had certainly started building a royal tomb in the Valley of the Kings since every king did this as soon as he came to the throne. Normally, the king's tomb was very big, with long corridors and several rooms leading to the burial chamber. All the walls were carved with scenes and texts and then painted. But when Tutankhamun died, Ay buried him in a small tomb not meant for a king. (Later Ay was buried in the tomb started for Tutankhamun.) Preparing the king's body for burial took 70 days, so Ay only had time to have the burial chamber painted. One of the scenes shows Ay as a priest performing important rituals at Tutankhamun's funeral. This was not a normal scene for royal tombs.

It was important for the next king to bury the one who had just died. Tutankhamun, though only a child, would have been, at least officially, in charge of the burial of Smenkhkare or Nefertiti. So to become the next king, Ay had to be in charge of Tutankhamun's funeral. He probably had the scene painted on the tomb's wall because he wanted to make sure that he got credit for burying Tutankhamun and got to be the next king. He might have chosen this particular scene because he really wasn't really supposed to be the next king.

A CT scan of Tutankhamun's skeleton shows that his spine was curved. However, the scientific team that studied the scan thinks this may just be the way the embalmers laid him out.

Work on the tomb might have been overseen by Maya, the treasurer and overseer of construction. While the tomb was being prepared, the dead king would have been taken to a place called the per-nefer, or beautiful house, where they mummified the body.

First, the internal organs were removed through a cut in the king's left side. Each organ (lungs, liver, intestine, and stomach) was dried, wrapped, and placed in a miniature coffin. These four coffins were placed inside a beautiful alabaster box with four lids, each in the shape of the king's head wearing the nemes headdress. This box had been made for another king—if you look closely, you can tell that the face on the stoppers and on the miniature coffins is not Tutankhamun's. The brain, which decays and becomes soft, was taken out through a hole made in the king's nose.

The body was then laid in a bed of natron, a salt that would dry it out and preserve it. After it had lain there for 40 days, the desiccated (dried out) body, now a mummy, was carefully wrapped in linen bandages, with jewelry and amulets placed on the body or wound into the wrappings. A beaded cap and a diadem (a crown with no top) were put on the king's head.

A golden mask, representing the king in his nemes

This miniature coffin from Tutankhamun's tomb held organs taken from the body during the embalming process.

These royal heads of Egyptian alabaster are part of the box that held the internal organs of Tutankhamun. They are stoppers and sit on top of the hollowed-out spaces inside the box where the viscera coffins (see picture on p. 53) were placed.

headdress, was placed over the king's head and shoulders. Tutankhamun's mask (see picture on p. 58) is one of the greatest masterpieces ever made. The face of the king is pure gold. His eyebrows are made of lapis lazuli, and his eyes are inlaid with white quartz and black obsidian. His ears are pierced for earrings. The stripes of the nemes headdress are represented by bands of gold and blue glass.

On the mask, Tutankhamun wears the divine beard of a god, also made of gold and lapis lazuli. On his forehead are the cobra of Lower Egypt and the vulture of Upper Egypt, who will protect him forever. The mask includes a collar—known to the ancient Egyptians as the *wesekh*—that covered the king's chest. On the back of the mask is a magical text. The writing connects the king with gods and goddesses such as Anubis, the jackal god of the cemetery; Re, the sun god; Horus, the hawk; Ptah-Sokar, a god of the dead; and others. Each god was supposed to play an important role in protecting King Tutankhamun against the dangers that he would face in his trip to the afterlife.

After the mask had been placed over the king's head, the priests said some prayers and covered the body and its mask with resin. The body, now prepared to last for eternity, was placed in a coffin of solid gold and taken on its final journey to the tomb.

We know from a picture of the funeral procession painted on one wall of the tomb that Tutankhamun's mummy was placed on a bed inside a shrine. All around the top of the shrine were carved images of cobras, which protected the king. Hanging on the shrine were garlands of flowers.

The shrine was placed on a wooden sled. This sled was pulled by the 12 most important officials of the king. The procession probably first went to the king's mortuary temple, near the edge of the flood plain. Either here or maybe at the tomb (nobody knows which), Ay, dressed in a special priest's outfit that included a leopard skin, conducted a ceremony that was part of a ritual called the Opening of the Mouth.

For this ceremony, the mummy (probably inside its coffin) was placed upright, and Ay touched the mouth, eyes, and nose with various implements. The Egyptians believed that the Opening of the Mouth ceremony restored the senses and made the mummy live again so that it could eat and drink and become a god.

There was probably a funerary meal, eaten by Tutankhamun's family and friends, that took place after the ceremony so that the king could share in the food. This might have

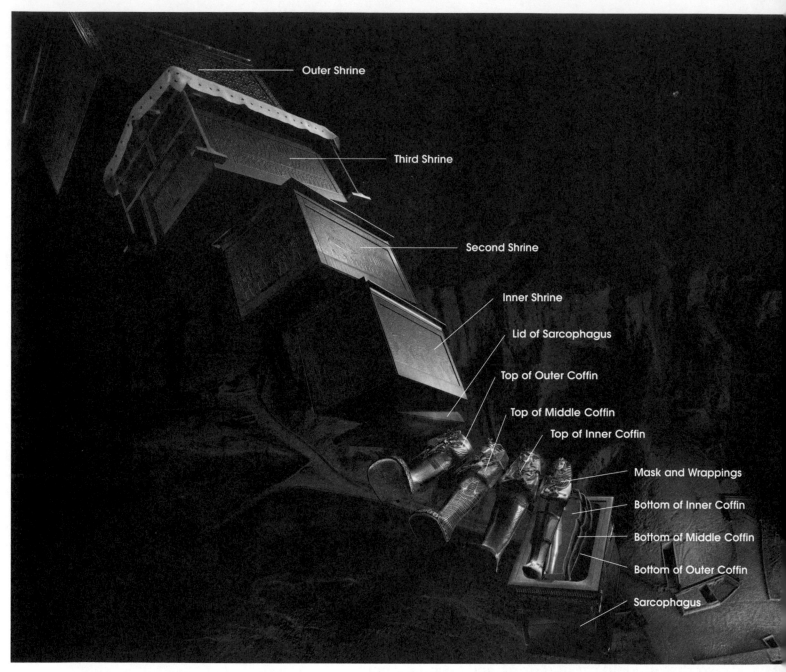

Outer Shrine

Third Shrine

Second Shrine

Inner Shrine

Lid of Sarcophagus

Top of Outer Coffin

Top of Middle Coffin

Top of Inner Coffin

Mask and Wrappings

Bottom of Inner Coffin

Bottom of Middle Coffin

Bottom of Outer Coffin

Sarcophagus

An artist shows all of the layers in which King Tut was buried. The mummy was wrapped, and a mask was laid over his head and shoulders. Then he was placed in a nest of three coffins, one inside the next. The coffins were put in a red quartzite sarcophagus. Then four nested boxes called shrines were built around the sarcophagus.

been at the tomb, perhaps in a tent set up outside. Remains of what might have been Tutankhamun's funerary meal were found buried in a pit near his tomb. Along with broken pottery vessels and floral collars were bundles of natron, which would have been used for embalming the king.

Either before or after the feast, the body was taken into the burial chamber. A nest of containers—two larger coffins and a stone sarcophagus—was waiting there to receive the body. The inner coffin was placed inside this nest. Then the lid of the second coffin, of wood covered with gold and inlaid with semiprecious stones, was closed. Next was the lid of the third coffin, similar to the second. Someone, who I like to think was Ankhsenamun, placed a wreath on the crown of this third coffin. I believe that the queen wanted to say farewell and to show her love for her dead husband.

Two sheets of linen were placed over this coffin, and the lid of the big rectangular stone sarcophagus was lowered into place. Then four gilded shrines were set up around the sarcophagus, one inside the next. The largest shrine filled most of the chamber. Sweeping away their footsteps behind them, the priests then closed and sealed the doors of the four shrines, one after the other.

We do not know if all of the objects buried with the king were already inside the tomb, or if they were brought as part of the funeral procession. Either way, the priests in charge would have made sure that all of the king's things were in place. Then the tomb was closed and sealed for eternity.

CHAPTER SIX

AFTER KING TUT

A t some point near the end of Tutankhamun's reign, perhaps just before or just after he died, the Egyptians seem to have lost the battle against the Hittites, and with it some of their empire. After her husband died, perhaps even while he was being mummified, Ankhsenamun sent a letter to the king of the Hittites. She asked him to send her a Hittite prince to marry since she had no son to make king and did not want to marry "a servant" (someone not of royal blood). She says in her letter that she is afraid.

The Hittite king did not believe her because no Egyptian princess or queen had ever married a foreigner. So he sent a messenger to Egypt to find out what was really happening. Ankhsenamun sent back another letter, along with an Egyptian messenger. The second letter said, "They say that you have many sons, so give me one of yours! He will be my husband, and he will be king of Egypt."

This was an amazing thing to say. We do not know why she wrote to the Hittite king. Maybe she didn't want to marry Ay and thought (or knew) that he had killed her husband.

The famous mask of King Tut. Crafted in gold, his young likeness is expressive and immortal.

Some people think that she was afraid that the Hittites would take over more of the Egyptian empire, maybe even going so far as to invade Egypt itself. If she was afraid of this, maybe she wanted to make peace first.

In any case, the Hittite king did send a son, but the prince died before he arrived in Egypt. The Hittite king was sure that his son had been murdered. If he was, the murder must have been ordered by someone with lots of power, like Ay or Horemheb.

The Hittite king was so angry that he attacked Egypt. He brought back prisoners, some of whom had a terrible disease. Many Hittites caught this disease from the prisoners and died. Not long ago, a team of archaeologists working at Amarna analyzed some material they had excavated and found microscopic traces of the Black Plague. This is probably the disease that the Hittites brought back with them.

We know that Ay buried Tutankhamun and became the next king. We are not sure what happened to Ankhsenamun after this. There is a ring of faience (made from crushed and melted pebbles of quartz) in Germany that has the name of Ankhsenamun next to the name of Ay. Just after the tomb of Tutankhamun was found, an Egyptologist saw a similar ring in a different color at a shop in Luxor. These rings probably mean that Ankhsenamun married Ay. I am sure she would have been very unhappy to marry this old man.

A beautiful statue was found in 1989 in the Luxor Temple. This statue shows a king and queen seated next to one another. The original inscription has been erased, but a scholar named Ray Johnson suggested that the king and queen might be Ay and Ankhsenamun. The queen is tall and thin, with very long, narrow fingers and a long, narrow face.

Ay was very old when he came to the throne, and he only ruled for three or four years. He had a son named Nakhtmin who was probably supposed to succeed him. But when Ay died, Horemheb finally became king. (A statue of Nakhtmin and his wife was found smashed, maybe by Horemheb's soldiers.) Horemheb ruled for about 25 years. During his rule, he began removing the memory of Akhenaten and his successors from history by tearing down their monuments and erasing their names. This was because Akhenaten was considered a heretic, someone who did not believe in the gods. Even though Tutankhamun had restored the old religion, his memory was destroyed also, and so was the memory of Ay.

The kings that came after Horemheb did forget about Tutankhamun, and they also forgot about his tomb. So did everyone else. Robbers got into the tomb twice in ancient times, probably soon after Tutankhamun was buried. But both times they stopped before they had taken very much. They stole mostly things that were easy to carry, such as jewelry and precious oils, and they never got into the burial chamber. If they had been caught, they would have been punished very severely, and probably even executed. Both times the necropolis police resealed the tomb, and 200 years later it was covered by the royal workmen of Ramses VI.

There the tomb lay, hidden under the sand and later rubble. All of the tombs around it were opened and robbed, but it lay quietly, waiting for the right moment to appear. And then Howard Carter came, and the name of Tutankhamun lived again. The greatest wish for every ancient

Seated statue of the god Amun protecting King Horemheb, successor of the aged king Ay. Horemheb was a high official and commander-in-chief of the army under Tutankhamun.

Egyptian was that his or her name would live forever. Tutankhamun's name and identity had been lost, but now he is one of the most famous kings in history.

After Carter and his team examined the body of Tutankhamun, it was put back into the tomb, inside one coffin and his large stone sarcophagus. He still lies there, visited by thousands of tourists each day. I worry about him there because his mummy is not in good condition. It was already in fairly bad shape when it was found, and no conservation has been done to it for over eighty years. I had thought about moving him to the Egyptian Museum in Cairo, but the journey would be too difficult. So we will carry out conservation in place, and let him rest where his loved ones left him so many years ago.

I believe, as an Egyptologist who has studied all the clues, that Tutankhamun might have died from an accident. But there are still things that we do not know and may never find out. Perhaps later we will find evidence that he was poisoned, or even that he died in battle. Some mysteries have been solved, but others remain. The life and death of the golden boy will always fascinate the world. The mystery will continue.

Time Line of Ancient Egyptian History

4500–3000 B.C. NEOLITHIC PERIOD
Agriculture is developed ▪ People are settled in villages with local rulers ▪ Egypt is made up of two regions: Lower Egypt, centered in the Nile Delta in the north, and Upper Egypt, along the river's course in the south.

3000–2650 B.C. EARLY DYNASTIC PERIOD (DYNASTIES 1-2)
Upper and Lower Egypt are united under one ruler with a capital at Memphis ▪ Egyptian scribes begin using hieroglyphics ▪ Royal tombs are built at Abydos and Saqqara.

2650–2150 B.C. OLD KINGDOM (DYNASTIES 3–6)
There are a strong central government and powerful rulers ▪ Trade and arts flourish ▪ The Step Pyramid of Djoser is built at Saqqara, the Great Pyramid of Khufu, other pyramids, and the Sphinx are built at Giza ▪ Kings' power declines toward the end of the period.

2150–2040 B.C. FIRST INTERMEDIATE PERIOD (DYNASTIES 7–11)
Drought, famine, and disease may have contributed to disorder ▪ The central government collapses, and Egypt is divided into separate warring kingdoms led by local rulers.

2040–1640 B.C. MIDDLE KINGDOM (DYNASTIES 11-13)
Mentuhotep II, fifth king of Dynasty 11, reunites ancient Egypt with a capital a little south of Memphis at Itj-Tawy ▪ Peace and prosperity return ▪ Thebes becomes an important town ▪ Rulers are strong and powerful ▪ Egypt conquers parts of Nubia (now Sudan) ▪ Kings are buried in pyramids.

1640–1550 B.C. SECOND INTERMEDIATE PERIOD (DYNASTIES 14-17)
Egypt again falls into disorder ▪ Foreigners known as Hyksos, probably from western Asia, take over the delta region of Lower Egypt and rule it for decades.

1539–1075 B.C. NEW KINGDOM (DYNASTIES 18–20)
Ahmose I of Thebes drives the Hyksos out of Egypt ▪ New territories are conquered and a great empire is built with capitals at Thebes and Memphis ▪ Egyptians enjoy great prosperity ▪ Burials are at the Valley of the Kings ▪ Tutankhamun is the third to last Pharaoh of the 18th dynasty.

1070–712 B.C. THIRD INTERMEDIATE PERIOD (DYNASTIES 21–25)
Widespread government corruption contributes to the collapse of the New Kingdom ▪ Egypt is divided into separate kingdoms ▪ Kings from Nubia (Sudan) and Libya rule during some of this period.

712–332 B.C. LATE PERIOD (DYNASTIES 26–31)
Assyrians from Asia invade Egypt and destroy its great cities ▪ Persians from what is now Iran conquer Egypt ▪ Last native Egyptian rulers are in power.

332 B.C.–A.D. 642 GRECO-ROMAN PERIOD
Alexander the Great of Macedonia, north of Greece, conquers the Persian Empire, including Egypt, in 332 B.C ▪ He founds the city of Alexandria in Egypt ▪ After Alexander's death, his general Ptolemy becomes king ▪ Egypt becomes a Roman province in 30 B.C.

More Books to Read

Berger, Melvin and Gilda Berger. *Mummies of the Pharaohs: Exploring the Valley of the Kings*. Washington, D.C.: National Geographic, 2001. This book, written for children 9-14, explores King Tut's tomb as well as the other tombs of the Valley of the Kings.

Brier, Bob. *The Murder of Tutankhamun*. New York: Putnam, 1998. The author of this book believes that Tutankhamun was murdered by Ay, and he tells you why. Although written mainly for adults, some older children will enjoy it.

Hawass, Zahi. *The Curse of the Pharaohs*. Washington: National Geographic, 2004. This book, written for children, tells about the curse of the pharaohs (which didn't really exist), and about my modern-day adventures with mummies.

Hawass, Zahi. *Secrets from the Sand*. New York: Abrams Books, 2002. This is the story of my life as an archaeologist.
It's written for adults but has lots of great pictures with captions that kids will enjoy.

Hawass, Zahi. *Valley of the Golden Mummies*. New York: Abrams Books, 2002. This is the story of my discoveries of a valley filled with tombs and mummies. Again, it's worth looking at for the many beautiful color photographs.

James, T.G.H. *Tutankhamun*. Cairo: American University in Cairo Press, 2000. This book has wonderful pictures of many of the objects from Tutankhamun's tomb.

Reeves, Nicholas. *The Complete Tutankhamun*. London: Thames and Hudson, 1990. This book (for adults) tells the story of Howard Carter, Lord Carnarvon, and the discovery of the tomb. It also has lots of information about the things found with the boy king, and a lot of pictures.

Smith, Stuart Tyson, Nancy Bernard, Brian Fagan. *The Valley of the Kings*. New York: Oxford University Press, 2002. This tells the story of the Valley. Written for children 9-12.

Index